TREASURES OF EGYPT

TREASURES OF EGYPT

AUGUST RAINES

CONTENTS

CHAPTER 1

Introduction to Egypt's Rich History

Egypt is a land of ancient wonders and modern marvels. This transcontinental nation spans both Africa and Asia, charming and intriguing countless generations year after year. Egypt's primary significance in the history of human civilization and natural history arises not only from its own varied and eventful past but also from its central position at the crossroads of many older cultures of the Afro-Eurasian mass, from the earliest Paleolithic settlements to the present day.

We marvel at the wonders of ancient Egypt in large part because they are the products not of sophisticated and learned eras, but of a now vanished Archaic Age. Its innocence, simplicity, and even primitiveness command more folkloric allure than most of the comparable achievements of relatively late civilizations like the Sumerians, the Minoans of Crete, or the Hittites of Asia Minor. These grand and ineffable structures, created by societies and cultures thoroughly enigmatic and mysterious, have always held a certain allure for a global audience. Their intensity reminds one of the almost supernatural hold which the age-old mystery religions of Osiris, Isis, and Serapis exerted over Alexandrians and even Romans during antiquity and right through early Christian times. Egypt's tombs have hidden countless treasures since the first pyramid was raided in antiquity. Even recently, gold with the image of an ancient Egyptian pharaoh was discovered in a Jerusalem parking lot.

The Importance of Egypt in Ancient Civilizations

Egypt, known officially as the Arab Republic of Egypt, is not just a transcontinental country that spans the northeast corner of Africa and southwest corner of Asia via the Sinai Peninsula, but it is also home to myriad ancient monuments. Besides the mesmerizing Nile River and the vast Sahara Desert, the most striking evidence of ancient civilizations exists within Egypt. Over 65 percent of the ancient treasures lie buried in the heart of Egypt, the cradle of magnificent landscapes, stupendous pyramids, perplexing tombs, wistful mummies, time-honored temples, and the ancient Egyptian kings resting in their gilded coffins.

Thanks to its remarkable stability, numerous wonders and marvels were built in Egypt during different civilizations and remain much talked about to this day. Despite the fact that the ancient Egyptians kept a written history of their great civilization over many centuries through inscriptions, the treasure trove and remains of this majestic civilization were discovered only recently. Notably, Petrie, who became an Egyptologist, excavated many of these sites, laying the foundation for understanding ancient Egypt. However, it was the discovery of a royal tomb at Thebes by American lawyer Theodore M. Davis in 1909 that made headlines. Wrathful at not making any further discoveries, Carter resigned from Davis's excavation. It was there, on November 4, 1922, in the Valley of the Kings, that Carter discovered the long-lost Egyptian tomb of Tutankhamun. Building on Petrie's work, Carter went on to become the single most important figure in Egyptology in the first half of the

20th century. His sense of responsibility towards preserving the heritage of ancient Egypt is unrivaled.

CHAPTER 2

Ancient Egyptian Architecture

Ancient Egyptian architecture is a breathtaking testament to the ingenuity and artistry of one of history's most remarkable civilizations. The ancient Egyptians left behind numerous architectural wonders, building magnificent stone temples and gigantic statues and constructing the only standing wonder of the ancient world: the Great Pyramid at Giza.

Today, over fifty pyramids can be visited in Egypt. These architectural marvels were built at a time when the Great Pyramid at Giza was the tallest man-made structure in the world for over 4,000 years. It's generally accepted that all the Egyptian pyramids were constructed using a core of stone blocks, which were then covered with Tura limestone blocks, using an outside (inward sloping) platform to pile up the blocks.

The pyramids were primarily constructed as tombs for the country's pharaohs and their consorts. Since the reign of the sixth pharaoh of the Third Dynasty of Egypt, Pharaoh Khufu (Cheops), the Giza pyramid complex has awed visitors. It's the only one of the ancient Wonders of the World that is largely preserved. You can visit the funeral complex of Giza Plateau through a combination of walks. The Great Pyramid of Giza is not only our most massive pyramid but also Islam's tallest pyramid. Built for Egypt's fourth Dynasty king Khufu (called Kheops by the Greeks), it stood originally at 480.6 feet (146.5 meters) high, but it is now some 450.7 feet (137.5 meters) in height. The base's side is 756.5 feet (230.4 meters) long, covering approximately 13 acres. When completed, the pyramid was covered with highly polished Tura limestone casing stones, which were later used to build mosques and fortifications in Cairo.

Pyramids: Tombs of the Pharaohs

The pyramids of Egypt are among the most instantly recognizable architectural sites on the planet. They've become a staple in popular culture, from the familiar gold-and-black constructs of board games to the cackling villains who dwell within their hand-hewn depths. These artifacts once served as the lynchpin of Pharaoh Pepi II's cult of personality. Despite their role in shaping public perceptions, the primary purpose of the pyramids was quite different: they were intended and used as tombs for the pharaohs of ancient Egypt, the area's God-Kings during the 3rd and 4th millenniums BC. Designed to secure wealth for the pharaohs in the afterlife and to keep safe the mummified remains of the deified ruler, the pyramids have served that function more than they did atop the Giza Plateau for the other seventy pharaohs of the dynasties.

For all their familiarity, these pharaonic mausolea have much to reveal. Egypt today boasts some 138 known pyramids, with their multifaceted functions reflecting the complex reigns of the pharaohs themselves. The step pyramids, with their six layers, may mimic the ascending and descending paths the cosmos offers, representing the myriad routes of transformation the dead pharaoh is free to explore. The step pyramid's richly decorated passages may reflect a mortal masquerading as a god, while the four thousand mastabas dotting the landscape across six millennia parallel the opportunities for personalization and customization for pharaohs, nobles, or townspeople.

Ancient Egyptian architecture, with its grandeur and complexity, continues to awe and inspire us, reminding us of a civilization that held such a profound understanding of both the material and the spiritual worlds.

CHAPTER 3

Art and Hieroglyphics

The ancient Egyptians' vibrant art scene was driven by their mastery of jewelry and ceramic statues, which they produced in abundance. The brighter the colors, the greater their value. For example, the elite class prized funeral cosmetic palettes, which were made of plastic and designed as birds, animals, or scenes like a hunter killing lions.

Ancient Egyptians immortalized their activities through hieroglyphs, artistic symbols representing words. These dramatic illustrations conveyed the power and might of the individual whose tomb or pyramid they adorned. Each painting was intended to guide the deceased through the trials of judgment and the afterlife. These images were believed to slay the deceased if the gods, and the scales and feather of truth, did not forgive them.

Famous Egyptian art includes the sphinxes of Tanis, now preserved in the Louvre. The stony maidens at Philae, with their fashionable long hair, reflect the refinement of the pharaonic age. The stunning murals from the burial chamber of Nefertari, near Thebes, showcase the religious connection between mummification and resurrection. Hieroglyphs could be written from right to left, left to right, or top to bottom, starting in any of the four corners. Pottery was fashioned at a distance, and scrolls of papyrus, which had cultural, economic, commercial, and political significance, were created. Ushabti statuettes, used to perform work in the afterlife, were particularly significant for the elite. These statuettes, amounting to as many as 365, were often stored in cupboard-like containers and affixed with spells from the "Book of the Dead" religious manual.

Symbolism and Meaning in Ancient Egyptian Art

Despite the diversity of media, functions, and sites, a common characteristic in ancient Egyptian art was the focus on visual clarity, uniformity, and stability of features, to the exclusion of naturalistic representation. The meaning was intended to be absolutely, universally, and eternally clear. Depictions of rulers adhered to codified poses and gestures, illustrating perceptions of order, stability, and divine approval. Certain images of animals, plants, and colors also carried strong traditional meanings.

Recent scholarship, particularly that focused on less "official" archaeological contexts, highlights the potential for complexity, multivalence, and change in the meanings of visual motifs and objects. According to these interpretations, individual images in a piece of Egyptian art could take on different significance in different contexts. Sometimes, works of art not produced to a uniform standard could silently express messages at odds with the official, sanctioned meaning. Furthermore, due to production, consumption, and adaptation complexities, individual artistic works could acquire meanings beyond those intended by their creators.

This section introduces major theories in the study of Egyptian art and explores attempts to describe and quantify idealized visual proportions and designs in two- and three-dimensional representations. While these studies often considered results to be deliberately conventional and unvarying in a social context, it might be possible to discern the visual characteristics deemed most pleasing and the basis by which the value of specific art objects in two and three dimensions could be determined and compared.

In addition, studies of production, reception, and adaptation have shed light on aspects of the endogenous meaning of Egyptian art. While individual artistic representations adhered to strict, idealized types, it's clear that interpreting general conventions requires sensitivity to smaller emphases on detail that were variable within accepted norms.

CHAPTER 4

Religion and Mythology

Egyptian religion has a long and continuous history, beginning in the predynastic era and continuing until the advent of Christianity in the 4th century C.E. At the center of religious and cultural life was Osiris, mythologized as a fertility god and associated with the Nile, agriculture, and time. It was believed that in life, all rivers flowed to Osiris, who in turn flowed into the living pharaoh, imparting his divinity to the king.

Religion permeated every facet of Egyptian society, including governmental, social, and economic activities. Massive state temples across the country served as centers of religious, political, and economic activity. Each temple was devoted to a primary deity and included elaborate rites and ceremonies to venerate the god.

The gods and goddesses of ancient Egypt exhibited a wide variety of essential characteristics and attributes. Some were represented with animal heads or the bodies of animals with human heads. For example, the hawks, falcons, and cattle kept on the temple grounds of Ra in Edfu were considered sacred. The ibis was a sacred animal to Thoth, and the mummified fish and skin of the cat Azrael were buried at a temple in present-day Turkey and Israel to signify their holiness. This religious mindset, bordering on the irrational or obsessive, was symbolized by the Hoeh, a well-known emblem from ancient Egypt, which was a round piece of metal with a stick-like hair on top. The Hoeh was the emblem of the ancient god Shu, related to the sun, air, and heavens.

The Pantheon of Egyptian Gods and Goddesses

The ancient Egyptians worshipped around 1,500 gods and goddesses, each responsible for a particular aspect of life and with different forms and manifestations. They believed that their gods and goddesses had created the world and overseen its existence since the beginning of time. Egyptian religion comprised a vast and elaborate set of myths, rituals, and symbols. They practiced regular religious ceremonies, though belief in the afterlife meant that most focused on preparation for the next world. All Egyptians would require the services of priests to help them achieve a place in the afterlife.

Osiris was one of the most important gods to the Egyptians. His yearly death and rebirth, symbolized by the rising and falling of the Nile, was a vitally important part of Egyptian religion. Osiris was equally associated with the values of the good king and the underworld. Horus, the son of Osiris and Isis, was associated with the living kingship of Egypt (the Pharaoh). Horus and Seth often appeared in myths as adversaries, with Seth attempting to murder and usurp Horus's position. There were many different gods and goddesses, each with unique authority, a specific name, icon, and mythology that identified them.

The gods and goddesses were not isolated from one another but were represented together. Their power and form were taken from the crown, the landscape, and the kings, as well as statues in temples for worship. As three-dimensional beings, they had a specific place in the temple, emphasizing their interconnectedness and the complex nature of Egyptian religion and mythology.

CHAPTER 5

Archaeological Discoveries

Egypt is home to many fascinating ancient tomb complexes, the most famous being the pyramids at Giza. The tomb of Tutankhamun, part of a complex of tombs in the Valley of the Kings, is also among the most renowned. Discovered by Howard Carter in 1922, the tomb and its treasures became international celebrities as some of the first extensive artifacts to be studied and publicly displayed in the 20th century.

Some tombs in the Valley of the Kings had been looted, their contents strewn throughout the shadowy corridors and chambers. However, some managed to avoid robbery through elaborate methods of concealment. It is argued that Tutankhamun's tomb withstood the ages by being hidden among the workmen's entrances to the tomb of Ramesses VI. The opening of another pharaoh's burial chamber had been walled up to mask the entrance to the burial of the boy-king.

The lavish treasures of Tutankhamun's burial were another great attraction. The Tomb of Tutankhamun has fascinated Egyptologists and the general public since its discovery in 1922, and it will continue to do so for generations. Advertisements featuring Tutankhamun graphics or his funerary mask on coffee cups or T-shirts are frequently found within the "Tombs of the Pharaohs" exhibit at the Oriental Institute of Chicago.

Excavations at The Workers' Village reveal how the workers who built the royal tombs in the Valley of the Kings and Queens lived. Nailbinding ring fragments, originally worn as finger ornaments, were kept by three Iraqi refugees and given to Geoffrey Huck, who was living in a compound in Jordan.

Tutankhamun's Tomb and Its Treasures

One of the most famous and extensive collections of treasures unearthed from an ancient tomb is that of Pharaoh Tutankhamun, who ruled Egypt during the 18th Dynasty, from c. 1336 until 1327 BCE. According to Howard Carter's description of the discovery and documentation of these objects in 1922, the majority of the items found in the tomb were ritual or funerary in nature. Most were either made or collected for King Tutankhamun at their point of production or use, though few dated to his reign.

The wealth of information about ancient Egyptian material culture accumulated through the study of Tutankhamun's tomb continues to deepen our appreciation of ancient Egyptian funerary art and daily life. In the Antechamber, some of the most important three-dimensional art pieces from the tomb were discovered, including the "Golden Throne," which is by far the best-preserved and most famous.

A study of the discovery sequence of the Antechamber's objects indicates that they were jumbled together, blocking all entrance doors, and were not found in a neat, labeled series of caches. Within this jumble, certain materials showed a clear preference for being near others, such as stone and metal, faience and gold. Dominating this space, as part of a coffin, gold masks and lithic sarcophagi were recorded.

In addition to these metal and textile artifacts, a young king's mummy was left, probably intentionally, near the entrance of the annex. To the right of the mummy, two stacked chests with partially together inscriptions were found, associated with funerary equipment, including beds and chairs. Many ritual scenes, most frequently depicting offerings, recur on the contents of these chests and other pieces of furniture from the tomb.

The detailed study and excavation of Tutankhamun's tomb have provided invaluable insights into ancient Egyptian culture, revealing the sophistication and artistry that characterized this remarkable civilization.

CHAPTER 6

Modern Egypt: A Blend of Tradition and Innovation

It's natural to assume that modern Egypt and ancient Egypt would be worlds apart. While there are several differences, the essence of Egypt in the modern and ancient worlds remains curiously similar. Modern Egypt offers a welcome blend of continuity with the past and dynamism, making it an incredibly interesting subject of study.

Indeed, every site in Egypt witnesses this harmonious coexistence of old and new. The City of the Dead, one of Cairo's oldest quarters, has residents who have lived in the centuries-old tombs of Mamluk and Ottoman nobles for hundreds of years. The Cave Churches of St. Samaan are an amazing blend of old and new beliefs. While many Coptic/Papyrus art shops aren't authentic, seeing mouth paintings still makes for a fascinating sight.

In Aswan, the Nubians are a living example of Egyptian tradition. The Nubian villages of Elephantine Island are popular with tourists for a touch of exoticism, but even better are the local food markets that tourists often miss. You can also visit a Nubian village by felucca (for a charge, of course). In Luxor, the most historical sites are near the ferry terminal. These sites still stand on their original ground, and you can visit local houses built into the ruins. The temples of Karnak and Luxor, just east of the ferry terminal, are always worth seeing.

The village next to the Temple of the Workers, behind the Colossi of Memnon, is dominated by the excavation, which recently yielded a workers' village representing the major Bohuric community of Deir el Medina. Just south of the pyramids, the village of Nazlet As Samaan was populated by tomb robbers. Now, it hosts visitors. Visiting these prairies truly showcases the progression of modern Egypt.

Cultural Preservation Efforts

Modernization and globalization pose enormous threats to the loss of cultural heritage. Efforts are being made at all levels of society to slow down or even reverse this erosion. The preservation of Egyptian historical heritage has shaped Egyptology into a full-fledged field of study. The governing principle of Egyptological research is "salvage of education, preservation," referring mostly to foreign experts who aim to prevent the loss of knowledge about Egyptian culture, now buried under millennia of sediment.

Nowadays, Egyptology is flourishing. The Egyptian people are showing increased interest in their heritage and take great pride in it. The government is doing a lot to preserve and restore ancient historical monuments and bring them to new light for future generations. However, much still needs to be done to raise public awareness about the grave threats facing some ancient Egyptian monuments and artifacts. Persuading professionals and leaders in economic, social, political, and international realms to make the right choices requires additional external support.

The most likely global candidates for activating such awareness are professional associations, international organizations, and forces that serve the global community, or at least have resources, attitudes, and operations relevant to the goals of memory and humanitarian need.

Modern Egypt's blend of tradition and innovation, combined with active cultural preservation efforts, continues to captivate scholars and tourists alike, ensuring that the legacy of this ancient civilization is not only remembered but thrives.

CHAPTER 7

Tourism in Egypt

Despite the presence of some of the world's most iconic and historically significant buildings, monuments, and artifacts, tourism in Egypt extends beyond these attractions and offers a host of other sites. Egypt is home to a rich and vibrant culture that has evolved over millennia. This culture is on display in various capacities across the country, particularly in major cities like Cairo and Alexandria, where dining, music, and history blend to tie the people of the past and present together.

The most famous of all Egypt's tourist attractions are the Sphinx and the pyramids at Giza. The Pyramid of Khufu, largest among the group and the second oldest of the Seven Wonders of the World, stands out. The ongoing battle to keep housing projects from encroaching on the ancient Nile adds to the challenges of preserving these historical sites. While modern developments around Cairo slightly encroach on these attractions, the motorways and commercial centers efficiently move people to and from these excavations and ruins, usually at affordable prices.

However, the burgeoning tourism industry in Egypt faces challenges. Several Nile tour operators have noted that the increase in tourist groups is swamping the more or less haphazardly managed ruins and museums. There is a legitimate concern about the ability of many sites to handle the continuously increasing tourist traffic.

Popular Sites and Attractions

Many of the most delightful and stimulating experiences in Egypt involve taking in the country's ancient glory. Scientific discoveries here are rewriting world history, and these wonders are not confined to museums; visitors can walk inside them, photograph them, and truly experience them. Egypt's ancient wonders are still very much a part of the living, breathing fabric of the country.

For history or culture buffs, Egypt is the promised land. Few places in the world allow you to see almost every great early civilization in one place. Pharaonic, Islamic, and Roman influences are everywhere, and each place you visit has the ability to surprise you.

If the Great Pyramid of Giza is the only archaeological site in Egypt you have heard of, then take a moment to reward yourself with a tour of the country's most fantastic sites. And if you already have an interest in ancient Egyptian history, such as the annals of Anubis and antique pharaohs, you will be in Pharaonic heaven here.

Egypt's ancient wonders embody civilization and are a proud expression of identity. These wonders, from mountaintop temples like Deir Bahaary to the gold mask-adorned faces of Tutankhamun and his family, are fascinating. They allow visitors to embark on a journey through time in one of the world's most beguiling destinations. Exploring the various corners of the country, you can truly experience the progression of modern Egypt.

CHAPTER 8

Egyptian Cuisine and Culinary Traditions

Egyptian cuisine is a rich mélange of African, Middle Eastern, and Mediterranean influences, full of simple spices and fresh ingredients. Influences from Greece, Persia, Rome, France, China, and India are also present in the food today. Historically, in the early days of civilization, animal husbandry was vital for ancient Egypt, making meat a key ingredient in the diet of both the lower and upper classes.

Bread and beer have remained staples in Egyptian life since ancient times. Bread, or "aysh," often made with garlic and various grains, was a basic food for most people. Beer, the main staple drink, was made from barley and had a bread-like taste, much like in Sudan today.

Egyptian cuisine employs simple cooking techniques, often using flavorful spices. It is a fabulous art form, offering a variety of flavors, textures, and aromas, and presents a feast for both the eyes and the taste buds. Though ancient Egyptians were predominantly vegetarians and meat was not widely available, a staple dish remains Koshari. This unique dish combines lentils, rice, and pasta, topped with a tomato-vinegar sauce.

Egyptian cuisine features a variety of fruits known for their fresh, light, and healthy flavors. Dates, guavas, mangoes, bananas, sweet limes (liums), coconuts, figs, cactus fruit (prickly pears), and many others are common. The pomegranate, famous for its intense crimson juice, along with the pear, is one of the most common design motifs in ancient Egyptian decorative art.

Key Ingredients and Dishes

The richness of Egyptian cuisine is reflected in its abundance of local produce. The primary ingredients that form the basis of most Egyptian dishes include lentils, rice, macaroni, bread, cakes, and macaroons. Olive oil and sugar are also essential, with olive oil used mainly for frying. Everyone may have their personal favorites among these dishes, but the variety is vast and inviting.

Some other key ingredients and dishes include:

- **Meat:** Despite being a predominantly vegetarian cuisine historically, meat dishes such as lamb, chicken, and beef are popular today.
- **Foul Medames:** A dish made from fava beans, seasoned with olive oil, garlic, and lemon juice.
- **Falafel:** Made from ground chickpeas or fava beans, deep-fried into patties.
- **Mulukhiyah:** A soup made from finely chopped jute leaves, cooked with garlic and coriander.
- **Mahshi:** Vegetables like zucchini, eggplant, and bell peppers stuffed with a mixture of rice, herbs, and sometimes meat.
- **Baklava:** A sweet pastry made of layers of filo dough filled with nuts and sweetened with syrup or honey.

The variety of meats, fruits, vegetables, and other ingredients used in Egyptian cuisine reflects the country's rich agricultural heritage and culinary traditions. Each dish offers a unique taste experience, showcasing the harmonious blend of flavors that characterize Egyptian cooking.

CHAPTER 9

The Nile River: Lifeline of Egypt

One of the most consequential symbols of ancient and modern Egyptian civilization is the Nile River. It is no mere decorative flourish; between its tropical origins and Arab terminus, it serves as a pulsating people-mover and water-whisk that conveniently curves through otherwise untamable deserts. The Nile River is Africa's largest and most enduring river, shaping Egypt's history, development, culture, and subsequent human settlement.

The Nile remains the lifeblood and lifeline of Egypt today, not only for the farming and transport it provides but also for the tangible existence of over 90 million Egyptians along its banks. Hard by the deserts where nothing grows, and scattered across landscapes where rainfall might only amount to one or two inches per year, the Nile is vital.

Egyptian civilization would simply not be possible without the Nile. This river flows through the realms of pharaohs and ancient cities, fostering one of the world's earliest literate city dwellers and helping tie together culture and religion across North Africa. Long after the ancient Greeks declared, "Egypt was the gift of the Nile," the river has continued to shape Egypt in significant ways. Today, it's useful to remember what power and import are carried through the length of the Nile. Perhaps over a quarter of Africa's population lives within the Nile basin, a vast region shared by eleven countries.

Historical and Modern Significance

The Nile River has always been the source of life for Egyptian civilization. Its deep impact is reflected in the rituals and mythology of the Egyptians. Though it is not as deep as before, the Nile still brings life to 80,000,000 Egyptians. The Egyptians have tilled their fields the same way they did 4,000 years ago for building dykes and farming. Rainfall was meager and unreliable, requiring help for a rich and complex civilization to sprout from the desert.

The historical significance of the Nile River and its consistent physical aspects are emphasized. In the present day, the river is still of great importance to Egypt and is seen as a "gift of the Nile." A wise man of the thirtieth century B.C. shared with Herodotus, "The country grows as the intricate fanning architecture of secular civilization, limited by the abundance and character of its waters and soils."

The Nile's mythology doesn't mean that sediments are still blocking the floodplain. But a tomato shoot can't thrive if it fully depends on rainfall. Life in early Egypt relied on sustaining and maintaining a reliable and regular flow of water to prosper. The Nile had a discharge of 60 million m^3/day before the delta split into the sea more than four thousand years ago.

The Nile's historical and modern significance continues to shape the region's culture, economy, and way of life, proving its enduring influence on one of the world's most fascinating civilizations.

CHAPTER 10

Literature and Intellectual Contributions

This section of the report provides a brief overview of the relationship between modern Egypt and Egyptian literature and ideas. Each of these topics could consume volumes and still maintain discussion, description, and evaluation. We have represented a variety of modern trends and counter-traditions, acknowledging the biases that may be evident in our selection. For instance, Northrop Frye has indicated a preference for Naguib Mahfouz, in part because his work is available in translation and incorporates French existentialism, Jungian myth, and Jacksonian/Sullivanian history. Our appreciation of Edwin Denby's encomia of the Tavistock Dictionary of Psychoanalysis (which is not available in the United States) is more limited.

Several other writers who could not be included in this section have also contributed significantly to Egyptian literature. Given the wealth of Egyptian intellectual contributions to the written word, its lack of context in an anthology of this size would have been inappropriate. It would be fascinating to include translations of works by famed historical intellectuals such as the Fathers of Christian

Egypt, the 13th-century Coptic-Arab chronicler al-Makin, or prolific modern contributors such as Lotfi Alkhouly, highly regarded as an essayist and cultural critic. These are potential subjects for future anthologies of Egyptian literature.

Famous Egyptian Writers and Thinkers

Ancient Egypt is known for its incredible art, luxurious lifestyle, advanced knowledge of the human body, and great pyramids. They also had a wonderful writing system. Sometimes they borrowed ideas or words from other writing systems, allowing us to read what ancient Egyptians wrote. Early Egyptian writers and thinkers include Djehuty, Kagemni, Neferirkare, Merikare, Amenemhat I, Ankhtifi, Nebkaure, Iseni, Akhenaten, Aper-el, Amenemope, Papyrus Harris I, Papyrus Wilbour, and Khali. The unearthing of books from the library of the royal palace of Tanis (residence of kings Osorkon and his successors - 22nd and 23rd dynasties) has done more to shed light on Egyptian literature than if all the temples and prowling places of the Delta had offered up their books filled with literary treasures.

Various treasures purchased from Gravi include religious texts, scientific works on the art of embalming, and inscribed stones recalling a king's famous deeds. The study of this papyri cache, supplemented gradually by different purchases and clandestine excavations, shed light on an ancient poem, the closest Egyptian equivalent of the Iliad or Odyssey. The opening scenes of the Tale of the Shipwrecked Mariner involve great officials accompanying the pharaoh to what appears to be a small lake, devoid of any Hellenistic influence, with clearly indicated lotus flowers pointing to a local tradition over a thousand years old.

For six days and seven nights, the pharaohs of the 12th and 19th dynasties were deeply moved by the tale of the shipwrecked mariner and forgot they were rulers of the earth, fascinated by the Adventures of the Shipwrecked Mariner. The Amenemhat carpenter's son contrasted at length, in 16 verses, his smiling youth with his current decrepitude, reminiscing about his covenants with various vassals in the southern provinces of Upper Egypt.

Egyptian literature and intellectual contributions have had a profound impact on the world, reflecting the richness of their culture and the depth of their thought. The legacy of these writers and thinkers continues to inspire and influence modern literature and ideas.

CHAPTER 11

Egyptian Music and Dance

Music was an integral part of all aspects of ancient Egyptian life. Both the music and the instruments of antiquity and today harken back thousands of years—the beat of Egyptian rhythm has remained the same! Keeping the traditions of the past alive, the Egyptian nights resound with the notes of folk music. The traditional **tahtib** is accompanied by the wonderful music from the reed-pipe, the **tala** (an instrument shaped like a pair of cymbals about 9 inches across and made of brass), and the **tabla** (also known as a **darabuka**—a little drum made of pottery and played with two sticks).

Though there are many various regions and cultures within Egypt, music and dance are two traditions that often rise to the top. Particularly where the Nile River meets the Mediterranean Sea, the traditions of dance and music date back thousands of years. Egyptians today pride themselves on music and dance that have deep roots in the past and continue to impact current and future generations.

A "tarha" is an Egyptian folk dance and is an example of this interaction between the old and new. Packed with rhymes, the tarha might describe one's love and lover, village, or anything else that comes to mind during one's performance. It starts with a conversation, and then by creating a little rhyme, the audience is welcomed to join in. Musicians around Egypt have their own versions, many using very basic instruments.

Traditional Instruments and Rhythms

Clapping and hands-on-legs beating may accompany this performance, and if singing is included, it is men who always do it since women will be dancing. Men might perform with the **Tanoura**, a special dervish dance, spinning around themselves a kind of skirt that continually changes color. The **Shamadan**, a big metal candlestick, is also a showpiece of Egyptian traditional dances. Egyptian music is characterized by its use of a large number of scales not used in Western music. The tetrachord, first preserved in the ancient Egyptian arched harp, exists in some of the music today. Another scale preserved in modern music is the Arabic pentatonic music.

Even Egyptian belly dance (**raqs sharqi**) is based on traditional music. This is the kind of music used for harem dancing recorded on manuscripts in various mausoleums throughout Cairo, Luxor, and Aswan. Dance pedagogue **Na'ila Mohamed** advises that there are five rhythmic patterns (**Iqa**) that underpin the basic tapestry of oriental dance. These patterns are the **Masmoudi Amad** (8 beats), **Baladi** (4/4), **Saidi** (4/4 a-spiked), **Malfuf** (2/4 with strides), **Maqsoum** (strict 4/4), and **Ayub** (2/4).

Baladi is unique because it is the most homophonic and unsyncopated of all Arabic music, yet its neutrality allows it to be accompanied by the other patterns. When teaching oriental dance, Na'ila also introduces these patterns and their respective techniques. Responding beat by beat, acceleration or slowdown from the knees, waist, and head while executing basic oriental dance footwork are the mystic aspects of basic dance technique that arise from the rhythms the dancer was weaned on.

Egyptian music and dance continue to play an essential role in the cultural fabric of the country, connecting modern Egyptians with their rich and vibrant heritage. The blend of traditional instruments, rhythms, and dance styles showcases the enduring legacy of ancient Egyptian art forms that have influenced generations and continue to captivate audiences worldwide.

CHAPTER 12

Contemporary Challenges and Opportunities

With its increasingly industrial character, Egypt faces immense environmental degradation, including desertification, loss of biodiversity, and modern threats accumulating due to dramatic population growth. The mounting pressures as Egyptians' needs for water, land, and resources conflict with the environmental needs. Urban development, quarrying, modern agriculture, and human visitation threaten archaeological sites in regions around Thebes in southern Egypt. However, programs such as the Tutankhamun Valley Project, aided by new technologies like satellite photography, offer the potential to limit some of these threats.

Modern tourism poses perils to both the landscape and ancient buildings. However, tourism's economic largess may offer opportunities for conservation. For example, creating protected areas contiguous with major tourist centers such as the Valley of the Kings, the Valley of the Queens at Thebes, and Dahshur near Cairo. Mounting concern regarding potential damage to these protected areas from excessive visitation has resulted in a national decree that geographic information systems (GIS) be instituted to "protect and conserve antiquities against destruction and loss so that visitors can enjoy them." The blueprint of such a system rests on the "collection of basic data, indices, analysis, and the production of topographic, geologic, archaeological, ecological, geographic, hydraulic, seismologic and other specialized maps of Egyptian deserts." A national symposium sponsored by the Egyptian Supreme Council of Antiquities and tourism industry leaders was convened in mid-April. Many proposals were advanced, including limiting visitation and leasing rights to sites to concessionaires.

Environmental Concerns and Conservation Efforts

Egypt may have more than its share of ancient treasures, but this phenomenal gift is also a great responsibility. The starkness of the desert accentuates the touristic value of the invaluable remnants from ancient history and highlights the necessity of conservation. Salinization, which has seriously affected the civilization of Southern Iraq, is already a problem in Egypt. It could become an enormous problem as more arable land is lost under the desert and fields have to be irrigated with increasingly concentrated Nile water. Waste disposal, pollution, increasingly dangerous pesticides, and other forms of pollution could render the most fertile land barren.

Industrialized nations may frown at 'do-not-develop-policies' when visiting such monuments, and the temptation exists to supply jobs and livelihood to the poor whose ancestors lived on some rock, preserved in raw desert squalor while watching tourists throw back empty Coca-Cola and Pepsi bottles. The possibility of sustainably managing these few selected sites with remote surveillance and protection from richer and less crowded countries is, at best, difficult and, at worst, ageist.

Balancing the grandeur of the monuments of Egypt with the needs of modern Egyptians is a delicate task. Conservation efforts must ensure that both the historical legacy and the current population's needs are met. Egypt's rich historical heritage demands careful preservation, but this must be balanced with sustainable development to support the country's growing population.

Efforts to raise awareness about the threats facing Egypt's cultural heritage are essential. Professional associations, international organizations, and global forces with relevant resources and operations are critical in activating such awareness. Balancing these efforts while ensuring the prosperity of modern Egypt presents a significant challenge and opportunity for both conservationists and policymakers.

CHAPTER 13

Conclusion: Preserving Egypt's Heritage for Future

The recording of inscriptions on the insides of the first pyramids reflects the ancient Egyptians' desire for their kings' achievements to be remembered. It is fitting to conclude by considering the value of the heritage of ancient Egypt—and indeed modern Egypt—for future generations. This reflection is not just a retrospective but a forward-looking mandate to preserve and honor the past while ensuring its legacy for the future.

Various scholars have highlighted the importance of preserving Egypt's cultural resources. Assmann (2020) envisages the Supreme Council of Antiquities' (SCA) plans for future cultural resources, consigning them to the desert's inscribed hills where today's Western world caught sight of ancient Egypt. Regulski (2020) considers the enduring legacy of what he terms the "Little Indiana Jones," while Zaloscer (2020) regards van Walsem's results as a continuation of a deep tradition of creating, collecting, and preserving images, forming our visual culture.

The purpose of the journal **Heritage Discovery**, for which this article was first written, is to provide a space for reflecting on the intersection of Egyptology and concerns about cultural heritage.

In their final reflections, the authors recount recent events to highlight concerns over the security of Egypt's finds and monuments. The exact situation is challenging to judge; major external websites still carry videos of streets submerged in Alexandria in January 2020. Whatever destruction of heritage, archaeological or architectural, caused or exacerbated by these and other floods in the last decade may be repaired by those working in presentation, curation, or museums.

Museums at home and abroad are rich in artifacts and records about Egypt. Field archaeologists and conservators will, and should, continue to uncover new artifacts and start new projects in the field, even in stricken locations.

Preserving Egypt's heritage is not just about keeping ancient artifacts safe; it involves a comprehensive effort to maintain the cultural and historical narratives that define this magnificent civilization. Efforts must be made to safeguard these treasures against natural and human-induced threats while educating future generations about their importance.

In summary, the preservation of Egypt's heritage for future generations is a multifaceted endeavor. It requires a blend of modern technology, international cooperation, and local commitment to ensure that the legacy of ancient Egypt continues to inspire and educate the world. The ongoing work of museums, archaeologists, conservators, and cultural heritage professionals is crucial in this mission, reflecting the timeless value of Egypt's contributions to human history.

www.ingramcontent.com/pod-product-compliance
Lightning Source LLC
Chambersburg PA
CBHW051502140726

47987CB00006B/2847